Caricature
and the Cartoonist

Peter Maddocks

ELM TREE BOOKS
LONDON

PUBLISHED BY THE PENGUIN GROUP
27, WRIGHTS LANE, LONDON W8 5TZ, ENGLAND
VIKING PENGUIN INC, 40 WEST 23rd STREET NEW YORK
NEW YORK 10010, USA.
PENGUIN BOOKS AUSTRALIA LTD. RINGWOOD, VICTORIA,
AUSTRALIA.
PENGUIN BOOKS CANADA LTD. 2801 JOHN STREET,
MARKHAM, ONTARIO, CANADA L3R 1B4.
PENGUIN BOOKS (N.Z) LTD, 182-190 WAIRAU ROAD,
AUCKLAND 10, NEW ZEALAND.

PENGUIN BOOKS LTD. REGISTERED OFFICES:
HARMONDSWORTH, MIDDLESEX, ENGLAND.

FIRST PUBLISHED IN GREAT BRITAIN
1989 BY ELM TREE BOOKS
COPYRIGHT C 1989 BY PETER MADDOCKS.
1 3 5 7 9 10 8 6 4 2

BRITISH LIBRARY CATALOGUING
IN PUBLICATION DATA
MADDOCKS, PETER, 1928 —
CARICATURE AND THE CARTOONIST
1. CARICATURES. TECHNIQUES
I. TITLE
741.5
ISBN 0-241-12676-2

·MADDOCKS.

HAVING TALKED TO MANY CARTOONISTS —
THE ONE THING THAT WE ALL AGREE ON AS FAR AS
CARICATURE IS CONCERNED IS THAT YOU EITHER
HAVE A GIFT FOR IT OR YOU HAVEN'T.
THOSE THAT DO HAVE THE KNACK ARE HEAD AND
SHOULDERS ABOVE EVERYONE ELSE (FIND FINE
EXAMPLES OF THEIR WORK WITHIN THE PAGES OF
THIS BOOK). THEY LEAVE THE REST OF US TO
STRUGGLE ON WITH A HIT HERE — AND A MISS
THERE...
CARICATURE IS AN ART, AN EYE FOR THAT
CERTAIN LOOK THAT GIVES US OUR OWN
PERSONALITY — MADE UP OF TWO EYES, A NOSE,
A MOUTH, A COUPLE OF EARS PUT TOGETHER
WITH THAT INNER SPARK SUPPLIED BY MOTHER
NATURE — IT'S THAT SPARK OR EXPRESSION
THAT THE CARICATURIST CAPTURES ON PAPER
CREATING A LIKENESS WE CAN ALL RECOGNISE.
        IF MY COLLEAGUES HAVE DONE THEIR
JOB (AND I ASSURE YOU THEY HAVE) AS YOU
FLICK THROUGH THE PAGES OF THIS BOOK
AND SPOT FAMILIAR FACES — THEIR
NAMES WILL IMMEDIATELY SPRING TO MIND
LIKE OLD FRIENDS THAT HAVE BEEN AROUND
FOR YEARS — THAT'S THE CARICATURIST
AT WORK...

·MADDOCKS·

I LOVE CARICATURE BUT I DO FIND IT A STRUGGLE —— I HAVE MY MOMENTS WHEN I CAN FIX THE PERSON I'M ABOUT TO DRAW FIRMLY IN MY MIND'S EYE AND SCRIBBLE AWAY WITH VERY REWARDING RESULTS —— OR A PARTICULARLY GOOD PHOTOGRAPH HANDS ME THE CARICATURE ON A PLATE. BUT I DO ENVY THE NATURAL CARICATURIST, WHO KNOWS EXACTLY WHAT HE'S DOING, WHAT LINE HE'S LOOKING FOR AND GETS IT DOWN ON PAPER SEEMINGLY WITHOUT EFFORT. ARTISTS LIKE GRIFFIN WHO HAVE A NATURALISTIC STYLE WHERE THE CHARACTER IS WHOLE SO THAT NOT ONLY CAN YOU RECOGNISE THE FACE — YOU ALSO KNOW THE STANCE OR POSE OF THE BODY...

OR GARY SMITH —
WITH HIS TECHNIQUE
OF USING DESIGN
SO THAT THE EYES
BECOME STARS OR
TRIANGLES AND HIS
DRAWING IS COMPLETED
NOT ONLY AS A CARICATURE
BUT ALSO A DESIGN OR
A SHAPE — I DO
ENVY THAT!

CHARLES GRIFFIN WORKS FROM SUNDAY THROUGH UNTIL THURSDAY EACH WEEK IN A TINY NARROW OFFICE OPPOSITE THE DAILY MIRROR BUILDING IN FETTER LANE, LONDON.
IN FRONT OF A WINDOW THAT RATIONED DAYLIGHT I LOVINGLY WALLOWED THROUGH A MOUNTAIN OF HIGHLY DETAILED PIECES OF ARTWORK TO MAKE MY SELECTION FOR THIS BOOK — BIG, GENEROUS SHEETS OF ARTWORK — CHARLES GRIFFIN DOESN'T WORK SMALL, HE LIKES TO DRAW EVERY WRINKLE THAT GOES INTO MAKING A FACE.

DIRECTOR

WHY DID A CARICATURIST TURN TO CARTOONING?—HE SAID HE WAS ONCE TOLD THAT CARICATURISTS WERE BUT A POOR RELATION OF THE CARTOONIST, AND THAT IF HE WANTED TO GET INTO THE FIRST DIVISION HE HAD BETTER DRAW CARTOONS. WELL—I FOR ONE AM PLEASED THAT HE DID COMBINE THE TWO AND GIVE US HIS UNIQUE STYLE—A STYLE THAT DOES NOT JUST GIVE US A FAMILIAR FACE STUCK ON SOME UNFAMILIAR BODY—BUT DRAWN AS ONE UNIT WITH AS MUCH DETAIL IN THE FINGERNAILS AS THERE IS IN THE FACE—HE ACHIEVES THIS BY WORKING OUT HIS CARTOON IDEA, THEN ROUGHING OUT THE ACTION OF THE CHARACTERS BEFORE HE GOES THROUGH HIS PHOTO FILE TO FIND A LOOK AND A GESTURE TO FIT HIS PENCIL ROUGH—AND THEN HE DRAWS IN THE DETAILED LIKENESS...

AND AS YOU CAN SEE — THE END RESULT
PAYS DIVIDENDS...A PERFECT COMBINATION.

I LOVE SERIOUS DRAWING, HE SAID. BUT I
ALWAYS WANTED TO BE A CARTOONIST AND WAS
GREATLY INFLUENCED BY CARL GILES OF THE
DAILY EXPRESS ——   I AM FASCINATED
BY HIS EYE FOR DETAIL, THERE IS ALWAYS
SOMETHING TO LOOK FOR IN HIS DRAWINGS.

GRIFFIN SAID HE LOVES TO DRAW WOMEN — PARTICULARLY THE TYPE THAT EAT THEIR MEN FOR BREAKFAST...

12"

18"

ORIGINAL SIZE

HE COLLECTS FAMOUS FACES LIKE SOME PEOPLE COLLECT STAMPS—— FILING THEM AWAY IN HIS CABINET FOR EASY ACCESS. IF YOU DON'T DO THIS YOU CAN WASTE A LOT OF VALUABLE DRAWING TIME—

SEARCHING FOR PICTURES IN THE LIBRARY, HE SAID—— DOING A DAILY CARTOON IN A NEWSPAPER NEEDS ORGANISATION ——— I'LL SECOND THAT, I SAID...

I WATCHED HIM DRAWING ON A LARGE SHEET OF SMOOTH COATED PAPER — I USED TO DRAW ON CARTRIDGE PAPER, HE SAID. BUT AS YOU CAN SEE I USE A FINE POINTED DIP PEN AND IT TENDS TO PICK UP THE SURFACE WHEN CROSS-HATCHING, SO NOW I ONLY USE THE SMOOTH SURFACE — ALSO IT TAKES PROCESS WHITE* AND I LIKE TO USE A LOT OF THAT.

I GET THE LIKENESS I WANT PURELY BY WORKING AT IT, I SCRIBBLE AWAY UNTIL I HAVE A FINISHED PENCIL DRAWING THAT I'M HAPPY WITH — THEN I START INKING IN. SOME FAMOUS FACES COME EASY——

BUT THERE ARE THOSE THAT DON'T.

THAT'S WHEN YOU START TO SWEAT!

* AN OPAQUE WHITE WATERCOLOUR PAINT FOR PAINTING OUT BLOTS OR MISTAKES

GRIFFIN USED TO DRAW HIS SCHOOLFRIENDS AT
SCHOOL FOR FUN — AND EVENTUALLY LEARNED
TO DRAW PROPERLY (HIS WORDS) AT HARROW
SCHOOL OF ART WHERE I HAD A VERY GOOD TUTOR,
HE SAID. HIS NATURALISTIC STYLE NOW DOMINATES
THE PAGES OF THE DAILY MIRROR —— THE CARTOON
BELOW STARTED LIFE AROUND TEN IN THE MORNING
AS AN IDEA. THEN FROM A PENCIL ROUGH AND THE
EDITOR'S APPROVAL, FOLLOWED BY PHOTOGRAPHIC
RESEARCH, HE STARTED DRAWING AROUND
LUNCHTIME TO FINISH READY FOR PUBLICATION
AROUND SIX THIRTY THAT EVENING.

TROG, OR WALLY FAWKES AS I REALLY KNOW HIM, SAYS
THAT IF YOU'RE A CARTOONIST, YOU KNOW ME AS THE ONE
WHO PLAYS THE CLARINET—— OR IF YOU'RE A MUSICIAN
I'M THE ONE WHO DRAWS CARTOONS, EITHER WAY,
HE'S GOOD. THE PITY IS WE CAN'T AFFORD TO SHOW
YOU HIS COLOUR CARICATURES (NOT IN A BOOK AT
THIS PRICE WE CAN'T). I THINK
THEY SHOW HIM AT HIS BEST,
HE HAS PRODUCED SOME
MAGNIFICENT 'PUNCH' COVERS
IN THE PAST—— HE TOLD ME
HE LIKED COLOUR BECAUSE YOU
CAN PLAY UNTIL THE HEAD STARTS
LOOKING BACK AT YOU — THEN
YOU KNOW YOU'RE GETTING
WARM — HOWEVER, HIS
PENMANSHIP IS A JOY TO LOOK
AT, SO YOU'RE GETTING YOUR
MONEY'S WORTH...

TROG WAS THE FIRST CARTOONIST REALLY TO
IDENTIFY MRS. THATCHER —THEN EVERYBODY
LATCHED ON TO WHAT HE CALLS 'THAT BIRD OF
PREY LOOK', THE HIGH BRIDGED NOSE AND HAWK-
LIKE EYES.

GEORGE MELLY, A FELLOW MUSICIAN AND WRITER OF
FLOOK, SAID: "TROG'S MRS THATCHER IS A USEFUL POINT
OF DEPARTURE WHEN CONSIDERING HIS APPROACH TO
CARICATURE. SHE IS SIMPLIFIED AS AN IMAGE,
REDUCED TO A FEW LINES — REAGAN TOO IS A
CARTOON-STRIP FIGURE, ON THE OTHER HAND...

LESSER-KNOWN POLITICAL FIGURES ARE DRAWN WITH NEAR-REALISM AND FREQUENTLY CROSS-HATCHED TO ACHIEVE SCULPTURAL SOLIDITY — THE LOGIC BEING THAT THATCHER AND REAGAN HAVE BECOME ALMOST ABSTRACT CREATURES, WHEREAS THOSE LESSER POLITICAL FIGURES REMAIN INDIVIDUALS AND ARE DEPICTED AS SUCH."
TROG SECONDED THIS, SAYING HE REMEMBERS BEING SORRY WHEN HATTERSLEY DIDN'T GET THE LABOUR LEADERSHIP, BECAUSE WE HAD ALL GOT HIM WORKED OUT TO PERFECTION — WE'RE STILL FIGHTING TO GET KINNOCK, HE SAID. WE CAN'T FIND HIM — THERE'S NOBODY IN!

HE ADMIRES DAVID LEVENE, THE AMERICAN.
A WONDERFUL ARTIST, I ADMIRE HIM
ABOVE ALL OTHERS —— THE BEST
CARICATURIST IN THE WORLD.
THE ONLY TIME HE FALLS DOWN
IS WHEN HE TACKLES A
BRITISH POLITICIAN, PERHAPS
LIKE WINE — SOME POLITICIANS
DON'T TRAVEL?

ALL TROG'S PORTRAITS
ARE DRAWN FROM
PHOTOGRAPHS IN
PEN AND INK——

RAYMOND BRIGGS, THE WRITER AND ILLUSTRATOR WROTE A FOREWORD TO FRANK WHITFORD'S BOOK ON TROG, TITLED 'FORTY GRAPHIC YEARS'——— "AFTER ALL HIS YEARS IN FLEET STREET WALLY FAWKES SEEMS NEVER TO HAVE FLAGGED THERE IS AN ASTONISHINGLY SHARP FOCUS IN HIS CARICATURE, MAKING HIS CHARACTERS SEEM LARGER THAN LIFE — THEN THERE IS THE QUALITY OF HIS BLACKS,

IT SEEMS TO BE BLACKER THAN BLACK. DOES HE USE THE SAME INK AS THE REST OF US? OR IS IT BECAUSE HE PLAYS THE CLARINET? PERHAPS HE HAS MORE WIND THAN WE DO?"

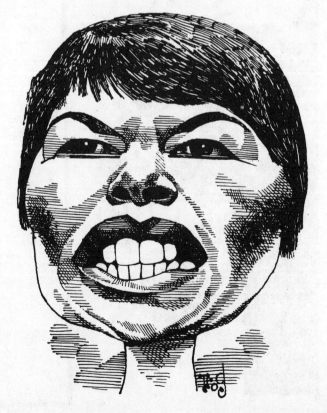

GARY

GARY SMITH IS TWENTY FOUR YEARS YOUNG,
SMALL IN STATURE AND VERY, VERY, TALENTED.
HE SAID, PEOPLE ARE ALWAYS A BIT DISAPPOINTED
WHEN I TURN UP IN PERSON— THEY SEEM TO EXPECT
TO MEET SOMEONE MORE FLAMBOYANT—YOU KNOW,
WITH A BLACK FELT HAT, ASTRAKHAN COAT AND A

LONG FLOWING SCARF,
BUT ALL THEY GET IS
ME IN JEANS AND A
TEE SHIRT—HE WAS
BORN IN PORTSMOUTH
AND NEVER THOUGHT
HE WOULD EVER EARN
A LIVING DRAWING
FACES...

I LIKED TO DRAW FACES AT SCHOOL AND WAS
ALWAYS GETTING INTO TROUBLE BECAUSE I'D
DRAWN MY TEACHER'S LIKENESS IN THE MARGINS
OF MY EXERCISE BOOK — EVEN THE ART TEACHER
(I DIDN'T GO TO ART SCHOOL) SAID I WAS WASTING MY
TIME DRAWING FACES — SO I WAS AMAZED WHEN
AT THE AGE OF EIGHTEEN THE LOCAL PORTSMOUTH
PAPER STARTED ME OFF BY NOT ONLY PUBLISHING
MY WORK, BUT PAYING ME MONEY FOR DOING
SOMETHING I ALWAYS LOVED DOING ANYWAY...

NOW I LIVE IN LONDON I LIKE TO WORK AT HOME, I WORK FLAT ON THE DESK SO THAT MY ARM IS FREE FOR THOSE FLOWING SWEEPING LINES. I PREFER A BRUSH BECAUSE I CAN VARY MY LINE MUCH MORE AND I LOVE THOSE SOLID BLACKS... I SEE THE FACE FIRST THEN I WORK IT UP INTO A DESIGN — NO, I DON'T STORE MUCH REFERENCE IT WOULD TAKE UP TOO MUCH SPACE, SO I USE THE PAPER'S PHOTOGRAPHIC LIBRARY, SOMETIMES THE SUNDAY TIMES SAY WHO THEY WANT AND SEND ME PHOTOGRAPHS.

I DRAW ON PAPER BECAUSE I FIND BOARD FAR TOO INHIBITING — YOU CAN WASTE PAPER BUT NOT BOARD — I DRAW QUITE LARGE BECAUSE I LIKE LOTS OF SPACE.

THESE DAYS THE TABLOIDS ARE TURNING TO COLOUR, I FIND THIS A BIT OF A PROBLEM BECAUSE I DON'T THINK COLOUR HELPS MY WORK TOO MUCH— I MUCH PREFER BLACK AND WHITE, IT HAS SO MUCH MORE IMPACT...

COLOUR IS FINE IF IT CONTRIBUTES TO THE WORK—TO GIVE AN EXAMPLE, YOU COULD NEVER IMAGINE BARBARA CARTLAND IN ANYTHING BUT PINK— SO COLOUR WOULD WORK WELL WITH HER CARICATURE...

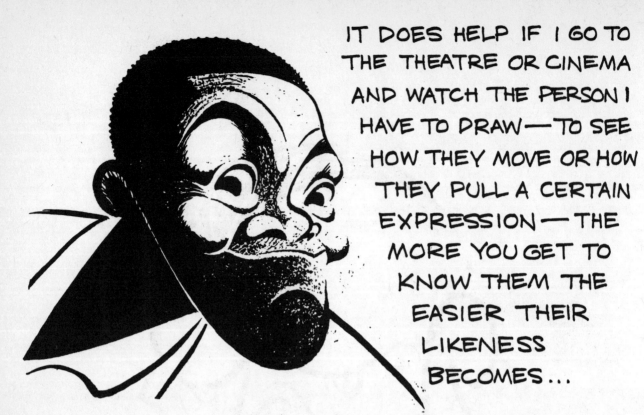

IT DOES HELP IF I GO TO THE THEATRE OR CINEMA AND WATCH THE PERSON I HAVE TO DRAW—TO SEE HOW THEY MOVE OR HOW THEY PULL A CERTAIN EXPRESSION—THE MORE YOU GET TO KNOW THEM THE EASIER THEIR LIKENESS BECOMES...

OF COURSE, TELEVISION IS A WONDERFUL WINDOW TO LOOK THROUGH, PARTICULARLY IF THE CHARACTER YOU HAVE BEEN ASKED TO DRAW HAPPENS TO BE ON THAT NIGHT—OR BETTER STILL IS IN A LONG RUNNING SERIES SO IF YOU MISSED THEM LAST NIGHT—THERE'S ALWAYS NEXT WEEK.

I NEVER REPEAT A DRAWING OF A SUBJECT NO
MATTER HOW MANY TIMES I DRAW THEM — I TRY
A DIFFERENT EXPRESSION WITH ANOTHER
ANGLE —— YET STILL KEEPING THEIR LIKENESS,
I FIND THAT A CHALLENGE.

I TRY TO INCLUDE HANDS, THEY ARE PART OF THE
DESIGN AND I ENJOY DRAWING THEM, I ALSO THINK
THEY HELP TO TELL A STORY — SOME POLITICIANS
MAKE GOOD USE OF THEIR HANDS. WINSTON
CHURCHILL HAD SMALL DELICATE HANDS, THE
OPPOSITE TO HIS STATURE — YET THE LATE
DAVID NIVEN WHO ALWAYS PLAYED THE
ENGLISH GENTLEMAN HAD STUMPY, BLUNT
FINGERED HANDS, QUITE DIFFERENT TO
THE IMAGE HE PORTRAYED ON THE SCREEN.

I USED TO MAKE THREE
DIMENSIONAL MODELS OF MY
CHARACTERS — THIS HELPED
ME TO GET TO SEE EVERY
ANGLE — BUT THESE DAYS
I JUST HAVEN'T GOT THE
TIME —— MAYBE LATER
ON I CAN GO BACK TO IT,
I HOPE SO...

I GOT A LETTER FROM AN ELDERLY
LADY WHO SAID SHE COULD TELL WHAT
MOOD I WAS IN BY MY DRAWINGS —
SHE ASKED ME FOR A SELF PORTRAIT,
AND THEN WROTE BACK TO ME
SAYING HOW SORRY SHE WAS FOR
THE WAY I LOOK.

SPITTING IMAGE

ROGER LAW OF THE FAMOUS 'FLUCK AND LAW' TEAM IS THE 'WALT DISNEY' OF THEIR LIMEHOUSE STUDIOS ON THE ISLE OF DOGS, LONDON —— SO SAYS, DAVID STOTEN, WHO, AT THE AGE OF TWENTY SIX IS THE SENIOR CARICATURIST IN CHARGE OF THE MODELLING BENCH.

HE CAME STRAIGHT FROM ART SCHOOL FOUR YEARS AGO TO TAKE OVER FROM TIM WATTS, WHO, AT THE TENDER AGE OF SEVENTEEN, WAS ONE OF THE PIONEERS OF SPITTING IMAGE WHEN THE SHOW STARTED BACK IN 1983 —— HE LEFT TO STUDY ART AT KINGSTON POLYTECHNIC. HE IS STILL A MEMBER OF THE TEAM...

OTHER MEMBERS OF THE TEAM ARE—PABLO BACH, A FINE CARICATURIST HERE ON A WORK PERMIT AND A RECOMMENDATION FROM FELLOW ARGENTINIAN OSCAR GRILLO, THE VERY BRILLIANT ANIMATOR.

STEVE MANSFIELD CAME FROM THE BBC SPECIAL EFFECTS DEPARTMENT (DR. WHO) AND HANDLES THE PAINTING, MOULDING AND MODELLING.
ALL DRAWINGS SHOWN ARE PENCIL/CRAYON WORKING DRAWINGS FROM THE TEAM...

DAVID STOTEN GAVE ME A GUIDED TOUR OF THE
STUDIO, SHOWING ME HOW THEY COLLECT MANY
NEWSPAPER AND MAGAZINE CUTTINGS OF THE
FAMOUS 'WE LIKE TO KEEP A CANDID CAMERA
COLLECTION OF THEIR EXPRESSIONS——BECAUSE
ONE ADVANTAGE WE HAVE OVER THE OTHER
ARTISTS IN YOUR BOOK IS THAT NOTHING HAS
TO GO TO PRINT——WE CAN WORK IN PENCIL AS
ROUGH AS WE LIKE TO GET THE LIKENESS, BUT
WE HAVE TO THINK THREE DIMENSIONAL...

'WE WORK OUT A PROFILE AND A FULL FACE DRAWING
AND PUT THEM TOGETHER WITH THE PHOTOGRAPHS.
THEN WE MODEL UP A LIKENESS IN WATER-BASED CLAY.
THE WORKING MODEL IS SMALL (ABOUT FOUR INCHES
HIGH) BUT THE FINISHED HEAD IS MUCH BIGGER,
LARGER THAN LIFE SIZE — ONCE EVERYBODY IS
HAPPY WITH THE FACE, WE MAKE A MOULD...

'TO MAKE A MOULD, WE HAVE TO ALLOW FOR A CHANNEL UP THROUGH THE HEAD SO THAT THE PUPPETEER'S ARM CAN GO IN TO WORK THE MOUTH. ALSO ALLOW ROOM FOR THE 'SKULL' MECHANISM THAT HOLDS THE EYES IN PLACE...

THE MOULD IS EITHER IN PLASTER OR FIBRE GLASS —IT DEPENDS ON WHAT KIND OF PUPPET IS REQUIRED. THE PLASTER MOULD IS THE SIMPLEST AND THE QUICKEST...

'WITH A PLASTER MOULD, WE USE A RUBBERY MATERIAL CALLED LATEX. WE JUST POUR IT INTO THE MOULD AND SWISH IT AROUND— THIS GIVES US A MATERIAL ABOUT THE THICKNESS OF A WELLINGTON BOOT. THE OTHER SYSTEM TAKES LONGER—WE USE A FIBRE GLASS MOULD AND INJECT FOAM INTO IT, THIS GIVES US A LONGER LASTING LUXURY PUPPET— BUT WHEN A WEEKLY SHOW IS GOING AT A RATE OF KNOTS, WE USE LATEX— THEN WE GO INTO THE FITTING ROOM FOR THE MECHANISM THAT WORKS THE EYES... WE HAVE TWO MOVEMENTS, THIS ONE, (IT LOOKED LIKE A PAIR OF SCISSORS ON THE END OF A TUBE) THIS WORKS THE EYE MOVEMENT, LEFT TO RIGHT OR RIGHT TO LEFT—AND THIS ONE — (A RUBBER BULB AGAIN ON THE END OF A TUBE) THIS IS THE BLINK...

'THERE ARE THREE
PEOPLE TO WORK ONE
PUPPET—THE PUPPETEER
WHO WORKS THE MOUTH
AND ONE ARM, ANOTHER
TO BE THE OTHER ARM
AND A THIRD TO OPERATE
THE EYES (USUALY
STANDING IN FRONT
OF THE ACTION—

SO THAT THE PUPPET
CAN REACT TO THE
DIALOGUE...'
I DON'T CARE WHAT
HE SAID—THEY STILL
LOOK LIKE REAL
PEOPLE TO
ME.

'SPITTING IMAGES'

Springs

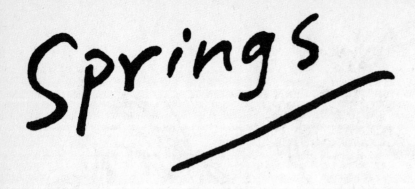

I MET JOHN SPRINGS WHERE HE WORKS — AT HIS HOME IN A BEAUTIFUL LEAFY SQUARE IN LONDON.

I SAID THAT HAVING STUDIED HIS CARICATURES FOR SOME TIME AS THEY APPEARED IN THE DAILY TELEGRAPH, I HAD COME TO THE CONCLUSION THAT HE WORKS INSIDE OUT.

— THAT'S EXACTLY HOW I WORK, HE SAID. I LIKE A GOOD BLACK AND WHITE PHOTOGRAPH OF MY SUBJECT, LIT FROM ABOVE IF POSSIBLE SO THAT IT SHOWS OFF EVERY LINE AND BLEMISH ON THE FACE. THEN I ALWAYS START ON THE LEFT EYE AND WORK MY WAY DOWN AND AROUND THE NOSE UNTIL I FINISH UP ON THE RIGHT EYE ——

BY THIS TIME I KNOW IF I HAVE CAPTURED THE
LIKENESS OR NOT——IF I'M HAPPY I CONTINUE
WITH ALL THE FINE DETAIL BEFORE I GO TO
THE OUTSIDE LINE OF THE FACE.
I USE A VERY FINE NIB ON MY PEN, I BUY
THEM BY THE BOX FUL AND I WANT TO
KEEP IT TO MYSELF BECAUSE MY NIB IS A
TRADE SECRET——FAIR ENOUGH, I SAID...

I USED TO INK STRAIGHT IN UNTIL RECENTLY, BUT NOW WITH TIME RESTRICTIONS AND DEADLINES I'VE STARTED TO PENCIL IN FIRST. JUST A VERY LIGHT LINE TO INDICATE THE LINE OF THE EYES OR THE SHAPE OF THE NOSTRIL——THEN I GO IN WITH THE PEN AND INK.   SIZE DOESN'T MATTER TO ME, THE DRAWING USUALLY DETERMINES ITSELF ANYWAY— SOMETIMES I GET SO ENTHUSIASTIC I RUN OUT OF PAPER SPACE AND HAVE TO STICK ON ANOTHER SHEET OF PAPER SO THAT I CAN FINISH THE DRAWING— THE TELEGRAPH PEOPLE ARE ALWAYS GIVING ME MEASUREMENTS TO FOLLOW

BUT I ALWAYS FORGET AND IT HAS TO BE ADJUSTED TO FIT THE PAGE... I'LL LEARN ONE DAY——BUT BEING SELF-TAUGHT IT'S THE DRAWING THAT MATTERS MOST TO ME.

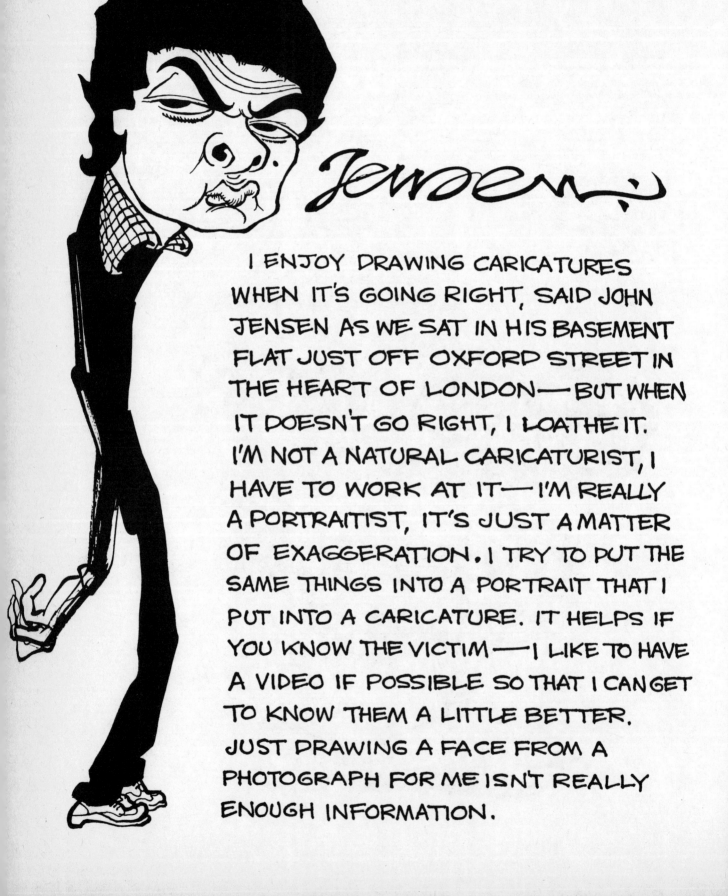

I ENJOY DRAWING CARICATURES
WHEN IT'S GOING RIGHT, SAID JOHN
JENSEN AS WE SAT IN HIS BASEMENT
FLAT JUST OFF OXFORD STREET IN
THE HEART OF LONDON— BUT WHEN
IT DOESN'T GO RIGHT, I LOATHE IT.
I'M NOT A NATURAL CARICATURIST, I
HAVE TO WORK AT IT— I'M REALLY
A PORTRAITIST, IT'S JUST A MATTER
OF EXAGGERATION. I TRY TO PUT THE
SAME THINGS INTO A PORTRAIT THAT I
PUT INTO A CARICATURE. IT HELPS IF
YOU KNOW THE VICTIM— I LIKE TO HAVE
A VIDEO IF POSSIBLE SO THAT I CAN GET
TO KNOW THEM A LITTLE BETTER.
JUST DRAWING A FACE FROM A
PHOTOGRAPH FOR ME ISN'T REALLY
ENOUGH INFORMATION.

———— MY DRAWING OF PAVAROTTI, ABOVE WAS ONE THAT WORKED BEAUTIFULLY—I SAT DOWN TO A BLANK PIECE OF PAPER AFTER WATCHING HIM BEING INTERVIEWED ON THE TELEVISION, AND WITH HIM FIXED FIRMLY IN MY MIND'S EYE —I DASHED OFF HIS LIKENESS WITH A FEW LINES, I FOUND THAT VERY SATISFYING——UNLIKE THE ONE I'VE BEEN WORKING ON THIS MORNING, IT'S SOMEBODY I DON'T KNOW, HAVE NEVER MET AND KNOW NOTHING ABOUT, ALL I HAVE IS A BLACK & WHITE PHOTOGRAPH. HOW MUCH EASIER THAT TROUBLESOME DRAWING WOULD BE, HE SAID. POINTING TO A PILE OF...

ROUGH SCRIBBLES ON THE FLOOR, IF I COULD SPEND ONE HOUR WITH THE SUBJECT IN REAL LIFE. SOMETIMES, NO PRICE IS WORTH THE EFFORT THAT GOES INTO A JOB—I'VE BEEN TWO DAYS ON THAT ONE AND I'M STILL A MILE AWAY FROM ANY LIKENESS...YUK!!

A LOT OF CARICATURE IN THIS
COUNTRY IT NOT WORTH THE
EFFORT—YOU CAN SCRIBBLE
AWAY DETERMINED TO GET THE
BEST LIKENESS YOU CAN IN
THE TIME AVAILABLE—IT CAN
TAKE MINUTES OR IT CAN
TAKE DAYS, ONLY TO BE
LOST IN THE COLUMNS
OF A NEWSPAPER AS
A THUMBNAIL SKETCH.
THAT'S THE BEAUTY
OF WORKING FOR PUNCH—
I KNOW WHAT I DO WILL
BE PRINTED AT A GOOD
SIZE ON GOOD QUALITY
PAPER—AND NOT LOOK
LIKE AN AFTERTHOUGHT
OR COLUMN FILLER.
I LOVE SPACE, I HATE
TO BE RESTRICTED TO
SIZE—GIVE ME PLENTY
OF ROOM FOR SOME GOOD
SOLID BLACKS, I SAY...

JOHN JENSEN WAS BORN IN AUSTRALIA,
THE CARTOONIST SON OF A CARTOONIST FATHER,
HE ARRIVED IN ENGLAND IN 1950. HE IS A GREAT
ADMIRER OF THE WORKS OF H.M.BATEMAN.
AND LIKE TROG CONSIDERS THE AMERICAN
CARICATURIST DAVID LEVENE AS THE BEST.
—UNFORTUNATELY HE HAS MANY COPYISTS
PRODUCING 'LOLLYPOP' TYPE DRAWINGS
CROSS-HATCHED TO DEATH!

MY ADVICE, HE SAYS.
IS TO CONCENTRATE
ON THE EYES AND
THE MOUTH—GET
THAT RIGHT AND THE
PERSON STARTS
LOOKING BACK
AT YOU...

R. 88 ← Willie Rushton

I WAS MORE OR LESS FORCED INTO CARICATURE, SAID WILLIE RUSHTON —— FILLING IN GAPS IN PRIVATE EYE MAGAZINE, I WAS OFFICIALLY ART EDITOR IN THOSE DAYS AND COULD ORDER PEOPLE ABOUT. I HADN'T GOT THE FAINTEST IDEA ABOUT LAYOUT SO I WAS DELIGHTED WHEN GERALD SCARFE CAME ALONG BECAUSE HE DRAWS SO BIG —— YES, I THINK I AM A NATURAL CARICATURIST BECAUSE I LOVE DRAWING FACES, THERE'S A STORY IN EVERY FACE, FORGET PALMISTRY OR CLAIRVOYANCY, ALL THE SECRETS ARE IN THE FACE.

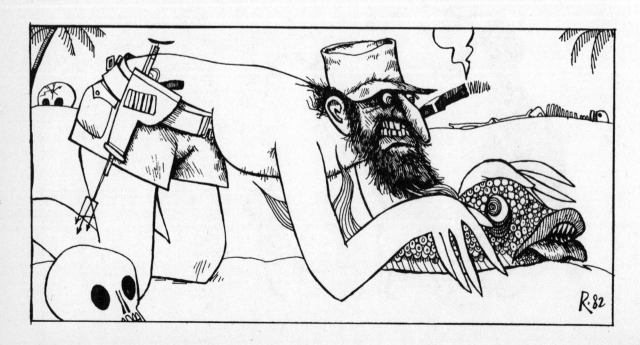

THE CARTOONIST USUALLY HAS TROUBLE GETTING
A LIKENESS INTO HIS STYLE, WHEREAS A
CARICATURIST IS NOT INHIBITED BY STYLE.
THERE ARE SOME LUCKY DEVILS WHO CAN
ACHIEVE IN SIX STROKES WHAT WOULD TAKE
ME A MORNING —— HOWEVER, I USED TO BE
FAMOUS FOR MY DRAWINGS OF FEET, I INVENTED
FEET, YOU KNOW — I USED TO GO AROUND
STUDYING PEOPLE'S SHOES, THESE DAYS I JUST
DRAW BLACK BLOBS AT THE END OF A TROUSER
LEG, AS I SAY I'M INTO FACES NOW ——
I'VE ALWAYS USED A PEN, I LOVE ALL THAT
CROSS-HATCHING, BESIDES, I COULD NEVER
GET ON WITH A BRUSH.

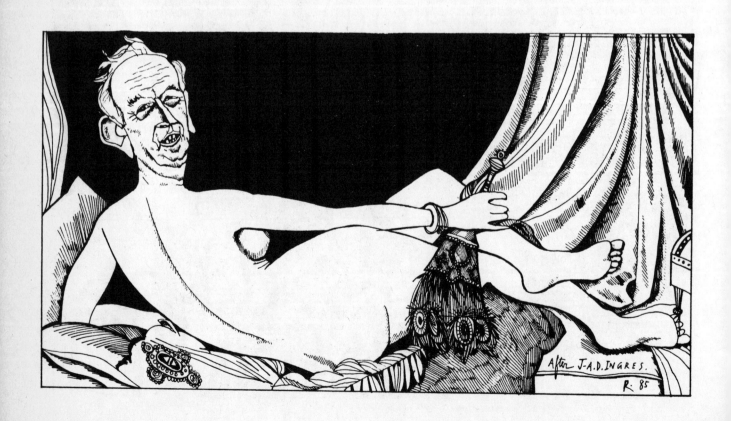

I USED TO JUST BASH STRAIGHT IN WITH PEN AND INK, BUT NOW IN MY OLD AGE I FIND A PENCIL LINE HELPS ME FIND THE LIKENESS, HOWEVER I NEVER JUST INK OVER THE PENCIL, BECAUSE IF YOU DO YOU WILL LOSE THE LIKENESS. I FIND I STILL HAVE TO CONCENTRATE ON THE PERSON WITH MY PEN AND JUST USE THE PENCIL LINE AS A GUIDE. SOMETIMES I DO AS MANY AS TWELVE FACES — AND THEN I CUT AND STICK THE ONE I LIKE BEST ON THE REST OF THE ARTWORK TO COMPLETE THE PICTURE. GOD BLESS TIPP-EX AND PRITT STICK I SAY, THE GREAT SAVIOURS OF CARTOONISTS.

———— I ASKED WILLIE RUSHTON WHY HE NEVER SIGNED HIS WORK?—— I DO, HE SAID, I PUT THE LETTER 'R' AND THE DATE.
IT GOES BACK TO THE EARLY DAYS OF PRIVATE EYE WHEN I WAS DOING SO MUCH WORK IT WAS EMBARRASSING TO SIGN MY NAME ON EVERY PIECE OF ARTWORK ON ALL THE PAGES OF THE MAGAZINE, SO I JUST USED THE LETTER 'R'——IT ALWAYS ANNOYS MICHAEL HEATH WHEN HE SEE'S IT —— WHY DON'T YOU SIGN IT? HE YELLS, OR AT LEAST CALL YOURSELF SPROD OR BOD OR SOMETHING —'R' IS JUST BORING!
I FIND THE DATE USEFUL, THAT WAY I ALWAYS CAN TELL IF I'VE IMPROVED OVER THE YEARS.

COLE

MY FATHER WAS AN ECCLESIASTICAL WOOD CARVER, SO I WAS VERY MUCH INFLUENCED BY HIS WORK, SAID RICHARD COLE, AS WE SAT DRINKING COFFEE AND NIBBLING 'DEADFLY' BISCUITS IN HIS RAMBLING LEAFY BACK GARDEN IN WIMBLEDON ON A WARM AUTUMN DAY...

I GREW UP SURROUNDED BY MY FATHER'S LARGE
WOODEN SCULPTURES — HE HAD TO STRUGGLE IN
HIS EARLY YEARS GOING WITHOUT HIS EVENING
MEAL TO GET TO EVENING CLASSES TO LEARN
HIS CRAFT, HE MADE SURE I HAD THE EDUCATION
HE NEVER HAD AND SENT ME TO WIMBLEDON
ART SCHOOL TO STUDY FINE ART. AFTER HE
DIED, I INHERITED HIS LOVE OF WOOD ALONG WITH
HIS WOODCARVING TOOLS...

First Ladies.

THERE IS A DISTINCT WOODCUT LOOK ABOUT
SOME OF MY CARICATURES, WHATEVER I DO,
THAT INFLUENCE IS ALWAYS LURKING IN THE
BACKGROUND. WHEN I FINISHED ART SCHOOL
I STUDIED TO BE A TEACHER, BECAUSE NO
MATTER WHAT YOU WANT TO DO IN ART— IT
PAYS TO HAVE A BACK-UP TO EARN YOUR
DAILY BREAD — WHILE I WAS TEACHING
ART I WAS ASKED TO DRAW BLACK & WHITE
ILLUSTRATIONS FOR A RECORD MAGAZINE
I HAD TAKEN SINCE I WAS SIXTEEN YEARS OLD.

I WAS GREATLY INFLUENCED BY THE GERMAN EXPRESSIONISTS, AND OF COURSE DAVID LEVENE. HE WENT BACK TO TENNIEL WITH HIS LOOSE CROSS HATCHING AND STILL REIGNS SUPREME IN THE SCRATCH AND HATCH BRIGADE...

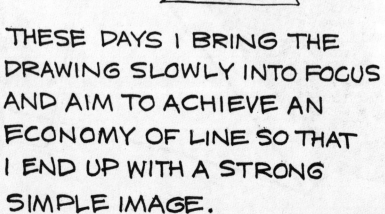

THESE DAYS I BRING THE DRAWING SLOWLY INTO FOCUS AND AIM TO ACHIEVE AN ECONOMY OF LINE SO THAT I END UP WITH A STRONG SIMPLE IMAGE.

I'M NOT SATISFIED WITH JUST DRAWING A CARICATURE,
I LIKE TO PUT AN IDEA INTO THE ARTWORK SO THAT
IT HAS SOMETHING TO SAY. IT'S SUCH AN EASY WAY
OUT JUST TO DRAW HEADS — I DROPPED ALL THAT
CROSS HATCHING AND STARTED DOING WOOD CUTS,
GOING BACK TO MY ROOTS. NOW I'M INTO FINE LINES
AND BLACK SHAPES — I LOVE SIMPLICITY THESE
DAYS, HOWEVER, I'M STILL LEARNING...

RICK BROOKES

I LOVE CARICATURE, BUT MY TROUBLE IS THAT MY ROUGHS ARE SO MUCH BETTER THAN MY FINISHED DRAWINGS, SAID RICK BROOKES OF THE LONDON EVENING STANDARD. I GET THE PHOTOGRAPHS OF THE SUBJECT FROM THE LIBRARY AND KNOCK OUT ABOUT SIX ROUGHS UNTIL I'M SATISFIED WITH THE LIKENESS.—THEN I START DRAWING IT IN INK AND WATCH IT GET LESS AND LESS LIKE THE PERSON. IT'S SO FRUSTRATING!

I WAS VERY MUCH INFLUENCED BY BERNARD PARTRIDGE IN PUNCH— AND OF COURSE DAVID LEVENE, I LOVE ALL THAT CROSS HATCHING, THAT'S THE BIT I ENJOY ONCE I'VE GOT OVER THE PAIN OF GETTING THE LIKENESS — THEN I CAN FILL MY FOUNTAIN PEN (IT'S A SWAN WITH A SPECIAL FLEXIBLE NIB)

AND I JUST SCRATCH AWAY TO MY HEART'S CONTENT. I DRAW QUITE LARGE, I CAN'T DRAW SMALL. CROSS HATCHING SUITS THE MALE FACE, IT CONTRIBUTES TO THAT RUGGED LOOK— UNLIKE THE FEMALE FACE WHERE YOU AGE THEM WITH EVERY SCRATCH...

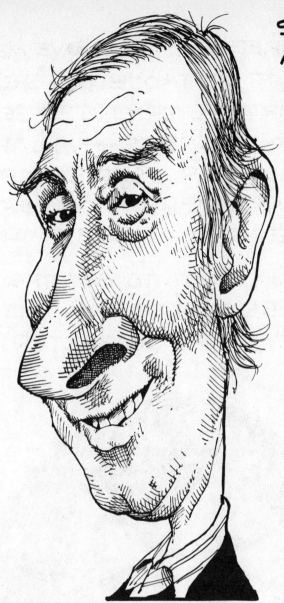

SOMETIMES I CAN REGISTER A FACE MENTALLY WHEN I MEET A PERSON. I HAD TO DRAW THE ACTOR DAVID TOMLINSON'S SON ONCE. WHEN I WAS INTRODUCED TO HIM HE WAS SO MUCH LIKE HIS FATHER THAT ALL I HAD TO DO WAS PULL OUT A PICTURE OF

TOMLINSON SENIOR FROM THE LIBRARY AND DRAW THAT — THE SON WAS SO PLEASED WITH IT HE TOLD EVERYBODY THAT I HAD A PHOTOGRAPHIC MEMORY, HE ONLY MET ME ONCE, HE SAID ——

MAUREEN LIPMAN GAVE ME A LOT OF TROUBLE, I SPENT FOUR DAYS TRYING TO GET HER LIKENESS — ALL THAT I GOT WAS A SERIES OF CHARACTERS FROM HER TELEVISION ADVERTISEMENTS.

YOU'VE GOT TO GET THE EYES RIGHT, THAT'S THE KEY TO THE CHARACTER...

PEOPLE TEND TO CHANGE THEIR LOOKS, THEY CUT THEIR HAIR OR GROW A BEARD — BUT AS LONG AS YOU'VE GOT THAT LOOK IN THEIR EYES — YOU'RE HOME AND DRY.

RICK BROOKES

Cummings

NOT ONLY HAVE I ALWAYS LIKED DRAWING—
I'VE ALWAYS LIKED DRAWING CARICATURES.
IT IS ALSO MY BELIEF THAT ANYONE INTERESTED
IN CARTOONING WILL FIND THAT CARICATURE
IS VERY MUCH A PART OF IT.
FOR A POLITICAL CARTOONIST LIKE MYSELF,
THE ABILITY TO MAKE MY POLITICAL
CARICATURES RECOGNISABLE IS ESSENTIAL.
I'VE ALWAYS GONE FOR THE STYLE OF
CARICATURE THAT IS AS SIMPLE AS
POSSIBLE—I HAVE NO TIME FOR THOSE
THAT TAKE CARICATURE TO EXTREMES,
SO THAT ONE HAS TO GUESS WHO
THE PERSON IS...

RECOGNITION OF A CHARACTER IN A CARTOON
MUST BE IMMEDIATE SO AS NOT TO CLOUD
THE MESSAGE OF THE FINISHED DRAWING.
I LIKE MY ARTWORK CLEAN AND OPEN—
NONE OF THAT FUSSY CROSS-
HATCHING WE OFTEN SEE.
IF I HAVE FIVE, SIX OR EVEN
SEVEN FAMOUS FACES TO
DRAW IN A LIMITED SPACE,
I BELEIVE IN USING THE
MINIMUM NUMBER OF LINES.
GOOD CLEAN LINES WITH
LOTS OF SOLID BLACKS
ARE THE ANSWER TO
NEWSPRINT...

YES, SOME POLITICIANS ARE EASIER TO DRAW THAN OTHERS — TAKE MR BREZHNEV, HE NOT ONLY LOOKED RUSSIAN, HE HAD THOSE WONDERFUL BUSHY EYEBROWS, UNLIKE MR GORBACHEV, HE'S A DIFFICULT ONE...

THE EMPTIES

THANK GOODNESS FOR HIS FAMOUS BIRTHMARK
ON THE TOP OF HIS HEAD — WE'VE GOT ANOTHER
TRICKY ONE WHEN MR BUSH BECOMES PRESIDENT
OF THE USA — HE'S GOT AN UNINTERESTING
FACE FROM A CARICATURISTS POINT OF VIEW,
THERE'S NOTHING THERE TO HANG YOUR PEN ON.
UNLIKE PRESIDENT REAGAN WHO HAS A
WONDERFUL FACE TO WORK WITH.
APART FROM HIS FRECKLES, NEIL KINNOCK
HAS GOT NOTHING GOING FOR HIM, IT'S A
RATHER BORING FACE. MY FAVOURITE AT
THE MOMENT IS NIGEL LAWSON, HE'S
GOD'S GIFT TO CARICATURE, HE'S AN
INSTANT CARTOON...

WHEN I SEE HEADLINES LIKE:
"NIGEL LAWSON FIGHTING FOR
HIS POLITICAL LIFE," OR "HOW
LONG WILL THE CHANCELLOR
LAST?"— I SHUDDER,
BECAUSE I DON'T WANT
TO LOSE HIM.
THE PROSPECT OF HAVING
TO DRAW CECIL PARKINSON
AS CHANCELLOR WORRIES
ME — WHAT WITH MR BUSH AS
PRESIDENT, MR GORBACHEV AND
CECIL PARKINSON — IT'S MAKING WORK!

THIRTY YEARS OF BUMBLING, FOOZLING, FRIVOLITY & SABOTAGE

THE UNIONS

Cummings

"HE stabbed the Pound!"

THERE'S A LOT TO BE SAID FOR HAVING A
WOMAN PRIME MINISTER WITH SHARP
FEATURES AND A NEAT AND TIDY HAIRDO.
SHE CREATES NO PROBLEMS—NOT TO ME
ANYWAY, PERHAPS IF SHE COULD GIVE
THE LEADER OF THE OPPOSITION A FEW
MORE WORRY LINES — I COULD MAKE HIM
LOOK A BIT MORE INTERESTING...

"It's his fault!"

Roy Ullyett

CARICATURE IS NOT AN EASY THING TO DO, BUT IT GETS EASIER THE MORE YOU WORK AT IT, SAYS ROY ULLYETT THE SPORTS CARTOONIST OF THE DAILY EXPRESS. WORKING TO A DEADLINE HELPS — YOU HAVEN'T GOT TIME TO SIT AND WORRY WHAT THE DRAWING IS GOING TO LOOK LIKE, YOU JUST GET ON WITH IT!

I DRAW WITH A BRUSH, SO IT'S ALWAYS DIFFICULT FOR ME TO FIND SOMEWHERE TO PUT MY INK — I'D TRAVEL TO A BIG FIGHT AND SIT AT THE RINGSIDE AT A RICKETY TABLE AND CHAIR AND THEN STRUGGLE TO CARICATURE TWO BLOKES THUMPING HELL OUT OF EACH OTHER WITH A HOWLING MOB BEHIND ME — ALL CALLING FOR BLOOD.

MY INK POT WOULD LEAVE THE TABLE EVERY TIME THE BELL RANG TO END A ROUND, THAT ALSO WARNED ME TO COVER MY ARTWORK AGAINST SWEAT, WATER, BLOOD AND HEAVEN'S KNOWS WHAT THAT SPRAYS AROUND A RINGSIDE BETWEEN ROUNDS.

SOMETIMES IT CAN BE JUST AS DANGEROUS OUTSIDE THE RING AS IT IS IN!

CRICKET GIVES YOU MORE TIME BECAUSE A TEST MATCH WILL LAST FIVE DAYS. I KNOW MOST OF THE CRICKETERS OFF BY HEART, SO I'VE GOT PLENTY OF TIME TO CONCENTRATE ON MY ARTWORK — BUT OF COURSE IF YOU'VE HANDED IN A CARTOON TO GO TO PRINT AND SOMETHING DRAMATIC HAPPENS TO CHANGE THE WHOLE SCENE — THEN YOU PANIC! THEY SAY A WEEK IS A LONG TIME IN POLITICS...

The one and only "GODDERS"

WELL I CAN TELL YOU A HALF-HOUR IN A SPORTS EVENT CAN MAKE ONE HELL OF A DIFFERENCE TO AN END RESULT. RACING IS ALWAYS A PLEASURE —

OVER THE YEARS I'VE GOT TO KNOW MOST OF THE JOCKEYS AND MOST OF THE HORSES ALL LOOK THE SAME TO ME —— BUT IT'S THE INTRODUCTION OF WOMEN JOCKEYS THAT GIVES ME A HEADACHE. GOLF IS MY FAVOURITE SPORT—AND THESE DAYS IS A PIECE OF CAKE, YOU JUST TELL THE PRESS OFFICER WHO YOU WANT TO TALK TO —HE BRINGS HIM TO THE INTERVIEW ROOM SO THAT HE CAN TELL YOU EVERY DETAIL OF EVERY STROKE WHILE I SIT AND SKETCH AWAY IN COMFORT—— NOT LIKE THE EARLY DAYS WHEN I HAD TO SEARCH THE FAIRWAYS TO FIND THE PLAYER I WANTED TO DRAW— THAT WAS HARD ON THE FEET.

©NICOLA

NICOLA JENNINGS IS AT THE AGE OF THIRTY
THE ONLY FEMALE CARICATURIST WORKING IN
FLEET STREET. I DON'T KNOW WHY, SHE SAYS.
NOTHING TO DO WITH ANYTHING SEXIST— IT'S JUST
WORKED OUT THAT WAY. I SEEM TO BE THE ONLY
ONE OF MY SEX INTERESTED IN DRAWING FACES.
I'VE ALWAYS STUDIED PEOPLE, WATCHED THEIR
EXPRESSIONS AND NOTED THEIR GESTURES—
AND JOTTED IT ALL DOWN ON PAPER...

I REMEMBER WHEN I WAS
AT SCHOOL I COULD
ALWAYS POKE FUN
AT MY FRIENDS IN
THE MARGINS OF
MY EXERCISE
BOOKS.
I WENT ON TO
WIMBLEDON ART
COLLEGE TO STUDY
THEATRE DESIGN
BUT DRIFTED BACK
INTO WHAT I LOVE BEST,
DRAWING CARICATURE...
I STARTED IN THE LONDON
DAILY NEWS WITH A REGULAR
DAILY SPOT UNTIL IT CLOSED...

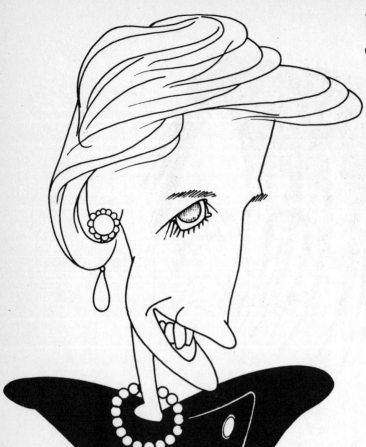

NOW I DRAW CARICATURES FOR THE T/V SLOT IN THE DAILY MIRROR AND I ALSO APPEAR IN THE SUNDAY TIMES — I ADMIRE THE WORK OF GERALD SCARFE, I LOVE THE WAY HE CAN STRETCH A LIKENESS — JUST TO THE POINT WHERE...

IT'S ABOUT TO VANISH AND THEN LEAVE IT JUST BALANCING ON THE EDGE. THAT'S WHAT I LIKE TO DO, SHE SAID. MAKING A MOVEMENT LIKE PULLING CANDY — STRETCH A FACE TO THE LIMIT AND SEE HOW FAR I CAN GO WITHOUT LOSING THE LIKENESS. BUT YOU NEED SPACE TO DO THAT —

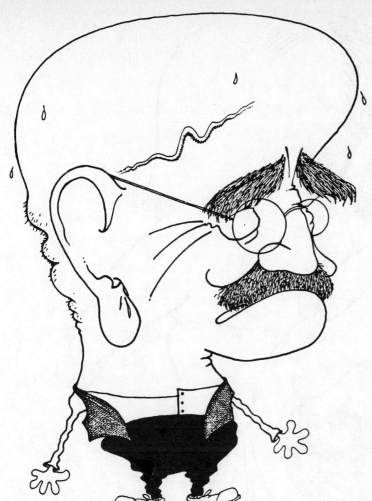

I'D LIKE TO TARGET THE POP WORLD WITH CARICATURE, POP PROMO'S AND ANIMATED TITLE SEQUENCES, THAT WOULD BE FUN — I'M REALLY JUST BEGINNING, AT THE MOMENT MY WORK IS PUBLISHED ABOUT THE SIZE OF A POSTAGE STAMP — I NEED SPACE TO SHOW WHAT I CAN DO. I WORK IN COLOUR OCCASIONALLY, BUT IT DOESN'T DO A LOT FOR CARICATURE — I MEAN, YOU CAN GIVE A PERSON WITH RED HAIR — RED HAIR...

CARICATURE REALLY DOES LOOK BETTER IN BLACK AND WHITE. I DRAW WITH A ROTRING PEN, I LIKE THE WAY IT CONTROLS A LINE. I DON'T DRAW TOO BIG, I LIKE IT TO FIT ON AN A4 SIZE — SOMETIMES I DO GET CARRIED AWAY...

AND YES, I'M PRETTY QUICK, SOMETIMES IT TAKES TEN MINUTES TO CAPTURE A LIKENESS FROM PHOTOGRAPHS — AND THEN THERE ARE THE ONES THAT TAKE THREE DAYS... HOWEVER, I DO LIKE A CHALLENGE.

ACKNOWLEDGEMENTS TO:

THE TIMES · THE GUARDIAN · THE STANDARD
THE DAILY EXPRESS · THE SUNDAY EXPRESS
THE DAILY MIRROR · THE DAILY TELEGRAPH
THE OBSERVER · THE SUN · THE DAILY MAIL
PUNCH · PRIVATE EYE · THE SUNDAY TIMES
THE MAIL ON SUNDAY ·

* AND MY THANKS TO ALL MY COLLEAGUES
FOR THEIR VALUABLE CONTRIBUTIONS

BRAVO

THANK YOU